9/6
SOP

Lyn

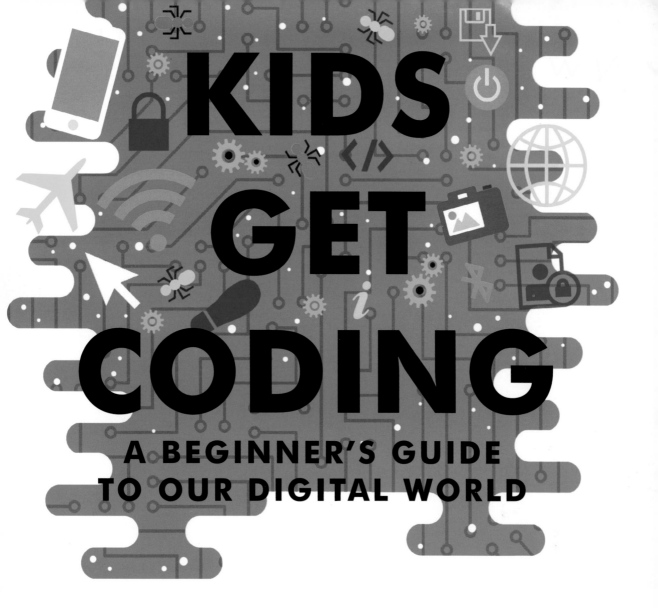

KIDS GET CODING

A BEGINNER'S GUIDE TO OUR DIGITAL WORLD

Heather Lyons & Elizabeth Tweedale

WAYLAND

Contents

Getting started

Hi! I'm Data Duck! We are going to learn about computers and how we can use them. Let's go!

We all use computers every day. Some computers we can see, and some are hidden inside everyday devices.

We will find out how to write computer programs and how to use them. We are also going to look at the parts of a computer, how they store information and how they follow instructions to do different jobs.

If we're going to be brilliant coders in the future, we need to understand the Internet. We'll discover what the Internet is, how to search it and how to stay safe online.

DATA DUCK

Here are some key terms you will learn about in this book. Try saying them out loud:

computer output pixel syntax

file byte metadata bug algorithm

program Internet password website

sequence search engine

loop

There are lots of activities in the book for you to try out. There are also some online activities for you to practise. For the online activities, go to **www.blueshiftcoding.com/kidsgetcoding** and look for the activity with the page number from the book.

Computers everywhere

Computers are all around us and come in many shapes and sizes. They help us do things, such as making phone calls, paying for groceries and doing schoolwork.

Computers are machines, so they aren't very smart on their own. They need instructions to be able to do their tasks.

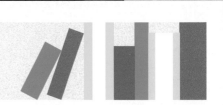

DATA DUCK

A computer's instructions are stored in its memory.

What can you see?

Can you spot five different types of computers on this page? What is each one used for?

Turn to page 76 to see the answers.

What can a computer do?

A computer is a type of machine. It can't think like us but it can store information and follow instructions.

Computers that have keyboards and screens are called laptops or desktops. Those that have touch screens are tablets or phones. There are also lots of other types of computers hidden inside everyday objects, like washing machines, music players or traffic lights.

Helpful machines

What are some of the things you do with a computer? Can you make a list like the one below?

- We can use computers to look up things on the Internet.

- We can use computers to write stories or draw pictures.

- We can use computers to help us with our maths homework and make graphs and charts.

DATA DUCK

When you start looking at the world around you, you quickly discover it is full of computers! Can you work out which devices near you have computers inside them, and which don't?

What is a program?

A program is a list of instructions that tells a computer what to do. The list is known as an algorithm. It is written in a language that computers can understand called 'code'.

Human brains can connect meaning to instructions. For example, if someone in the playground said, "Go down the slide", we would understand that they mean for us to first walk up the steps, then sit and slide down.

However, a computer needs step-by-step instructions:

1. Walk to the steps.
2. Climb up the steps.
3. Sit at the top of the slide.
4. Slide down the slide.

Robot walk

Pretend a friend is a robot and write down a set of instructions that he has to follow to walk in a square.

Were your instructions clear enough? How could you have made them clearer?

DATA DUCK

Remember, the robot can only understand the exact instructions you give him: nothing more and nothing less.

What is an algorithm?

'Algorithm' sounds like a big word, but it just means a series of steps, like those of a recipe.

Computers use algorithms to complete all the tasks we need them to do. We have to give computers clear instructions in the algorithms, so they understand what to do.

5. Brush top and bottom teeth for 2 minutes.

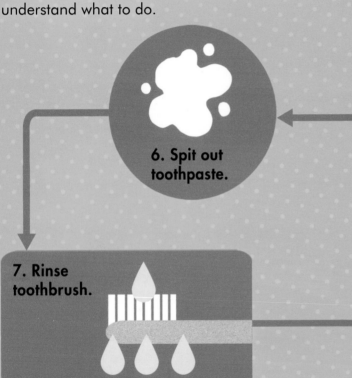

6. Spit out toothpaste.

7. Rinse toothbrush.

8. Put toothbrush back in holder.

DATA DUCK

A computer will use an algorithm to play a movie, search the Internet or make a phone call.

We use algorithms to do all sorts of everyday jobs. An algorithm for brushing our teeth might look something like this:

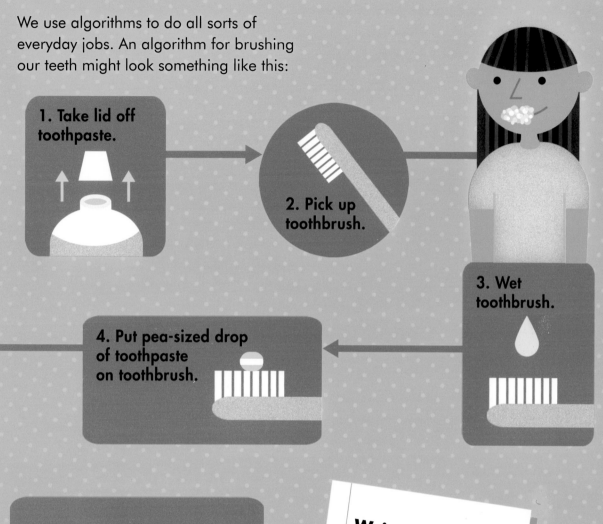

1. Take lid off toothpaste.

2. Pick up toothbrush.

3. Wet toothbrush.

4. Put pea-sized drop of toothpaste on toothbrush.

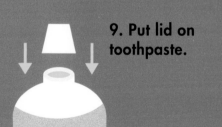

9. Put lid on toothpaste.

Write your own algorithm

Try and write an algorithm for getting ready for school. You'll need to think about all the things you do from the time you wake up to the time you leave your house.

Turn to page 76 to see the answers.

Order, order!

The steps of an algorithm need to be in the correct order for it to work. The order of steps in an algorithm is called a sequence.

When we write an algorithm, we have to get the sequence of steps right. When we get dressed, for example, it would be silly if we were to put on our shoes before our socks!

DATA DUCK
If the steps of an algorithm are in the wrong order, it won't work!

Cookie algorithm

Data Duck has written an algorithm to help him make his favourite chocolate chip cookies, but he's got the order of the steps all mixed up. Can you put them in the correct order?

Turn to page 76 to see the answers.

Mix together the butter and sugar, then add in eggs and flour.

OFF

Turn off oven.

Grease baking tray.

Put spoonfuls of mixture on to tray, then bake for 10 minutes.

Eat and enjoy!

Heat oven to correct temperature.

180°

Computer languages

Computers use different languages, just like humans all around the world do. Computers need the code for programs to be written in a language they can understand.

The language **HTML** is used to show web pages on the Internet. Computers use programs called Internet browsers (like Safari, Chrome or Firefox) that understand HTML.

Scratch was written for kids to help them make their own computer programs. It uses blocks that we can snap together to build instruction lists.

Python is used to search for things on the Internet, and to organise all the information that a computer keeps in its memory.

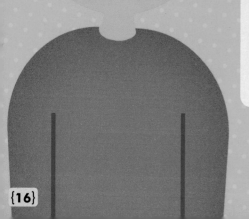

Java can be used to do some of the same things as Python. It can also be used for making computer games and apps.

DATA DUCK

A computer programmer needs to write the program in the best language for the job it needs to do. For example, Python is better at organising information and HTML is better at displaying it on a web page.

Mix and match

The way programmers use different computer languages is similar to the way people doing certain jobs need specific kinds of instructions. Can you match the instruction books below to the person who needs them?

Turn to page 76 to see the answers.

TASTY DISHES

MEDICAL DICTIONARY

FIXING CARS

HOW TO BUILD A HOUSE

Rules to follow

Computer languages use lots of symbols, letters and numbers. These fit together in a special way so that computers understand them.

A computer programmer needs to follow a set of rules known as the 'syntax' when writing a program. The syntax explains how the symbols, letters and numbers are put together. If anything is wrong in the code, the computer will get confused and will not know what to do.

```
print("Happy Birthday")
```

This Python code will write the words 'Happy Birthday' on the computer screen. For the text to appear on the screen, it must be in brackets and must have speech marks around it.

( )

brackets

" "

speech marks

Hello, World!

The computer languages below will all show, "Hello, World!" on the screen. Which parts of the code are the same? Which symbols are used in the syntax of each language?

Turn to page 76 to see the answers.

HELLO, WORLD!

HTML:
```
<BODY>
<P>
"Hello, World!"
</P>
</BODY>
```

Python:
```
print("Hello, World!")
```

Java:
```
public class HelloWorld
{
 public static void main(String[]args)
 {
  System.out.println("Hello, World!");
 }
}
```

Scratch:
```
when clicked

say Hello, World! for 2 sec
```

IF, THEN and ELSE

Simple computer programs can also make complex decisions. A computer programmer will use 'IF statements' in the algorithm so that computers can make a decision.

We can use IF statements to decide what to wear in the morning:

IF it is rainy, THEN wear wellies.

We can use the same IF statement to tell the computer to choose between two options:

IF it is rainy, THEN wear wellies, ELSE wear sandals.

Computer programmers use flow charts to plan decisions in programs. Here is one that helps you decide what to wear. This is based on the IF statement above.

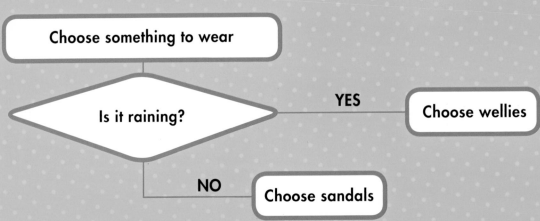

Choose something to wear

Is it raining?

YES — Choose wellies

NO — Choose sandals

School dinners

Look at the flow chart below. Can you decide which of the meal options below should be in the last two boxes?

Turn to page 76 to see the answers.

DATA DUCK
ELSE is the computer's word meaning 'otherwise'.

Choose your meal

Do I want a cold meal?

YES

Do I want a meat-free meal?

YES → Which meal fits here?

NO → Which meal fits here?

Cheese sandwich

Roast chicken

Macaroni and cheese

Ham and potato salad

CEREAL-O'S

Make a move

We can write computer programs that move pictures around the screen.

When we animate a character on a computer, we use code in the algorithm to tell the computer where the character should be on the screen.

To make the character move, we need to change its position over and over again.

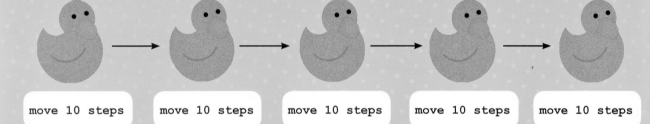

move 10 steps → move 10 steps → move 10 steps → move 10 steps → move 10 steps

DATA DUCK
The things that we can change in the algorithm, such as size, colour and position, are called variables.

If we want to change a character's colour, size or position, we have to change the code.

Spot the variables

Look closely at these two pictures.
Can you find four different
variables in the second picture?
Use this list to help you:

position

costume

size

rotation

movement

Turn to page 76 to see the answers.

For more variable fun, and to have a go at creating your own algorithm to make Data Duck move, complete the activity found at: **www.blueshiftcoding.com/kidsgetcoding**

Moving around

When computer programmers want to move characters or objects around a screen, they need to give location instructions as part of the algorithm.

The computer thinks of the screen like a map grid, so we need to tell the computer how the characters should move around the grid.

Let's use this treasure map to practise!

Treasure hunt

Data Duck has been blindfolded by pirates and needs your help to get to the treasure!

You can give him four instructions:
- Move left (by some squares)
- Move right (by some squares)
- Move up (by some squares)
- Move down (by some squares)

For example, to get to a duckling you would say:

Move right 5 squares

Move up 1 square

Turn to page 76 to see the answers.

Using the commands on page 24, see if you can complete these treasure challenges. Good luck, me hearties!

1. Get to the treasure (avoid the pirates and the snake).
2. Get to the treasure, collecting two ducklings along the way.
3. Get to the treasure, collecting two ducklings and going under the bridge.
4. Get to the treasure, collecting two ducklings and going across the bridge.

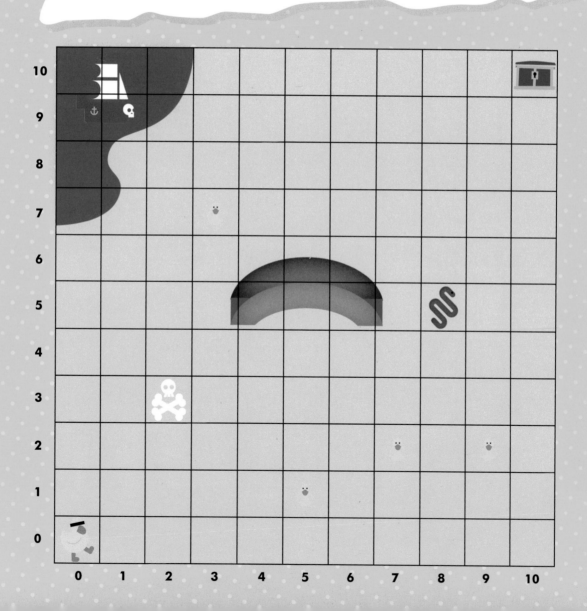

Giving instructions

When we write an algorithm, we need to think carefully about what we need it to do. The computer will need an instruction for every step that we can think of.

One of the instructions we need to give is where everything needs to go. Let's say we want to program a robot to feed our dog. We need to think through all the questions below so that we know all of the instructions to give the robot:

When does the dog eat?
How much does the dog eat?
What does the dog eat?
What does the dog eat out of?
Where does the dog eat?

When we have answered all the questions, we can start building an algorithm like the one below:

At 3pm, put one scoop of Bark-o's in plastic bowl on the kitchen floor.

If we leave anything out, the program will go wrong and the dog will be hungry!

Robots are computers, so they can't see and understand things the way we do. We need to tell the robot where to find everything. One of the ways we can tell the robot where to find things is with 'co-ordinates'.

Co-ordinates tell computers exactly where things are. Co-ordinates have two numbers: an 'x' number and a 'y' number. The 'x' numbers go across the map and the 'y' numbers go up and down the map. When giving locations, we always say the 'x' number first, then the 'y'.

Map the dog!

Here is a map of the dog, his bowl, his food and the robot.

The robot is at $x = -240$, $y = 0$

Where is the food?
Where is the bowl?
Where is the dog?

Turn to page 76 to see the answers.

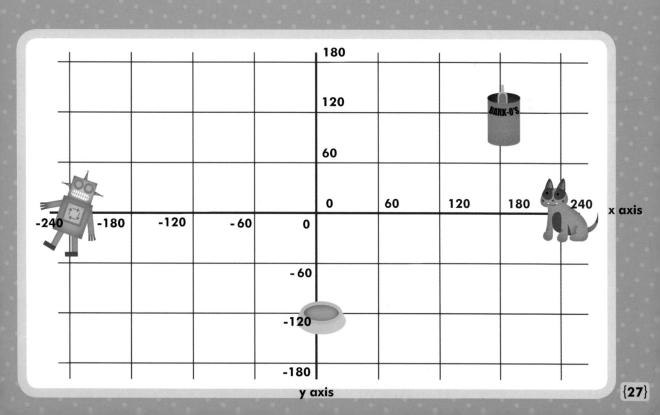

Writing a program

Now we know how to give a computer both detailed instructions and specific locations, we can write a program!

Apple picking

Data Duck has decided to go apple picking. Can you write down which of the steps on the right he needs to follow to pick three apples for his lunch?

Turn to page 76 to see the answers.

Go to x=120, y=-180

Go to x=-240, y=-60

Go to x=-180, y=120

Go to x=120, y=0

Pick up basket

Put apple in basket

Go to x=-120, y=60

Go to x=60, y=120

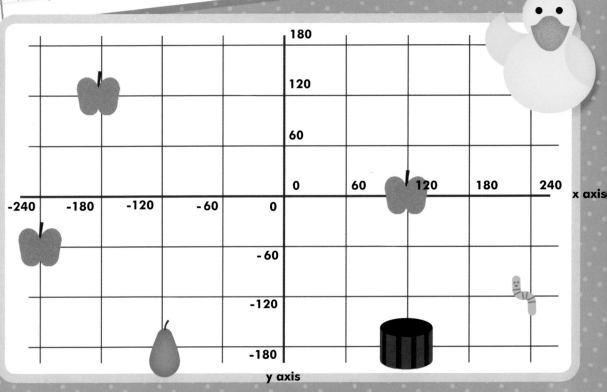

Go to **blueshiftcoding.com/kidsgetcoding** for more fun helping Data Duck go apple picking.

Sometimes, we need computers to do a task over and over again. We call these sorts of instructions 'loops'.

We repeat tasks every day. When we walk to school, we repeatedly put one foot in front of the other. When we pedal our bikes, we move our feet round and round. To tell a computer to do these things, we can use loops.

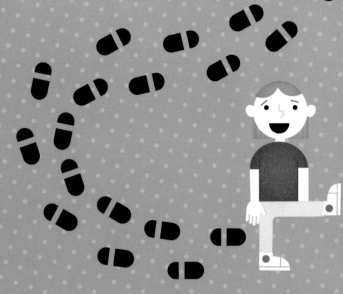

DATA DUCK

We use loops whenever there's an action or instruction we want to repeat, for example if I want to walk all the way across the screen.

On page 22, we had to tell the duck to 'move 10 steps' five times to get it to move across the page. Another way to do this is to put one instruction inside a loop, like below:

```
repeat 4 times

move 10 steps
```

Go to **blueshiftcoding.com/kidsgetcoding** for more practice with loops!

Predict it

It's helpful if we can predict what an algorithm is meant to be doing before asking the computer to complete the instruction.

When we press play on a video, for example, we expect a movie to start. But if the steps are in the wrong order, it won't work!

Look at the algorithms below. Can we predict what will happen to Data Duck if we give him the following instructions?

> change size by one-tenth smaller

> rotate by quarter-turn

He's going to become smaller, and twist around by a quarter-turn.

Now, can we predict what will happen if we change the algorithm again?

repeat 4 times
> change size by one-tenth smaller

> rotate by quarter-turn

He'll make the same movement as the first – but four times! He's going to get smaller four times, and turn four quarter-turns.

Guess the shape

Can you predict what shape Data Duck is drawing?

Repeat 4 times
    Move 4 steps
        Make a quarter-turn

Turn to page 76 to see the answers.

Now, have a go at writing your own instructions to draw:

a cross shape

a T-shape   an L-shape

Can a friend guess the shape by following your instructions?

Catching the bug

Algorithms are very useful, but sometimes they don't work and we need to find out why. Problems with algorithms are called 'bugs'.

When a programmer reads through an algorithm to find errors and fix them, it is called debugging. Errors might be a missing step or part of the sequence in the wrong order.

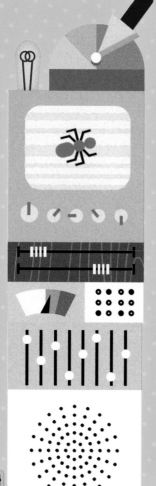

DATA DUCK
When computers were first invented, they were enormous! One day, one of these big computers wouldn't work. When scientists took it apart, they found a moth inside! Some people say this is why we use the word computer 'bug'.

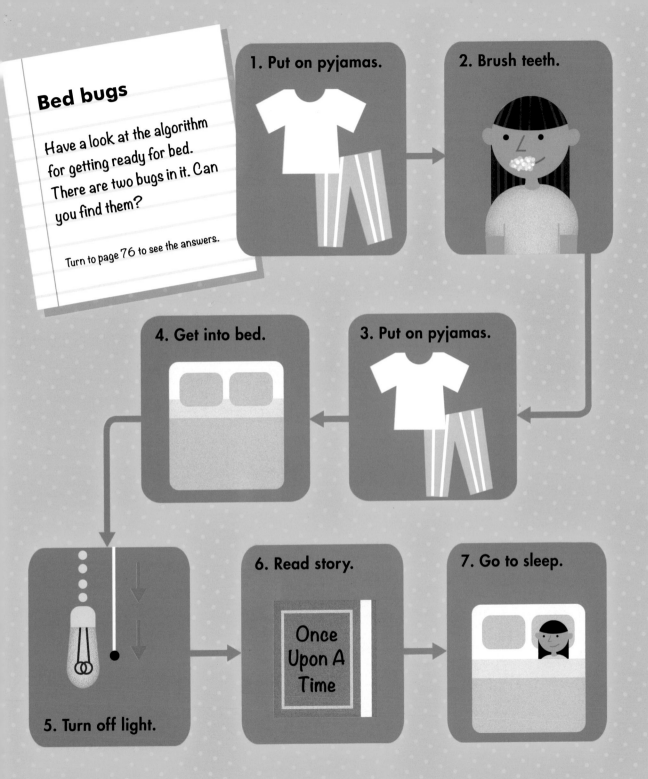

Bed bugs

Have a look at the algorithm for getting ready for bed. There are two bugs in it. Can you find them?

Turn to page 76 to see the answers.

1. Put on pyjamas.

2. Brush teeth.

3. Put on pyjamas.

4. Get into bed.

5. Turn off light.

6. Read story.

Once Upon A Time

7. Go to sleep.

Go to **blueshiftcoding.com/kidsgetcoding** and look at the debugging exercises for more practice.

Problem solving

When writing programs, a computer programmer needs to predict what the program is going to do, before the computer does it.

Look and find

Look at the following computer programs. What will the Python program draw? What will the boat do in the Scratch program?

Turn to page 76 to see the answers.

```
Go To (0,0)
Pen Down
Go To (2,-3)
Go To (-2,-3)
Go To (0,0)
Pen Up
```

Hint: try to work it out on graph paper.

```
when clicked
repeat until space bar pressed
    glide 1 sec to x: 100, y: 0
    glide 1 sec to x: -100, y: 0
```

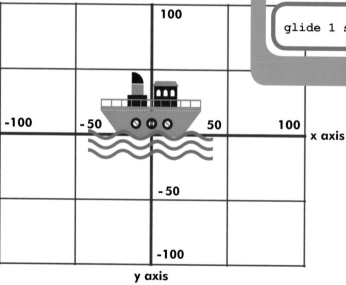

Bug hunter

It's also important for programmers to look at code and find bugs.

Look at the following computer programs. They are almost identical, but a few sneaky differences have appeared in the bottom program.

Can you spot these four bugs?

Turn to page 76 to see the answers.

```
When I receive a message
say Hello
ask What's your name?
forever
    turn 15 degrees
    move 10 steps
```

```
When I receive a message
say Hello
ask What's your age?
repeat 10 times
    turn 51 degrees
    move -10 steps
```

Go to **blueshiftcoding.com/kidsgetcoding** for more debugging challenges.

Exploring the digital world

Computers can help us do a lot of different things. We can make and keep sounds, pictures and videos on our computers.

We are going to look at the parts of a computer, how they store information and how they follow instructions to do different jobs.

DATA DUCK

How do we store a file?

DATA DUCK

Do computers have brains?

DATA DUCK

How do we find a file on our computer?

We will learn how to make sounds and pictures on our computers.

DATA DUCK

Here are some key words you will learn about in this section. Try saying them out loud:

computers   input   output   pixel

file   bit   byte   metadata

megabyte   gigabyte   terabyte

Inputs and outputs

There are many different parts to a computer. Some parts store information and other parts let us see and hear information.

Camera
This puts information about what the computer 'sees' into the computer, so it is an input device.

Processor and memory
Computers store files and programs in their memory. When we give a computer instructions, the processor (which is a bit like a brain) follows them and shows us information on the screen. It is not an input or an output device.

Screen
This is an output device. Programs use the computer screen to display information.

Keyboard
The keyboard is used to put information into the computer: it is an input device.

Mouse
We use the mouse to select things on the screen or to move them around. It is also an input device.

Speaker
Information (sound) comes out of the speaker, so it is an output device.

DATA DUCK

An input device is what we use to send information into the computer. An output device is what we use to see or hear information sent out from the computer.

In or out?

The kids on this page are all doing different activities. Can you decide who is putting information into the computer (input) and who is receiving information from the computer (output)?

Turn to page 76 to see the answers.

All kinds of content

Computers can store school presentations, music, movies, stories, pictures and games. Just about anything! These things are all different types of digital content.

Computers store and save things in a file. We then need special programs (sometimes called 'applications') to open these files and look at the content.

There are special programs for every sort of content: programs for reading and writing words, for looking at pictures, for watching videos or listening to music, and even for browsing the Internet.

Different types of files have different letters at the end of their names. These letters tell us what kind of file they are and what kind of program can open them. Some of the letters you may have seen include:

.html (a web page)

.pdf (a document with pictures and words)

.doc (a Word document)

.jpeg (a picture)

DATA DUCK

These letters at the end of a filename are called extensions.

Matching

In the green boxes are types of content. In the red boxes are sorts of programs. Can you match the right program with the right content?

Turn to page 76 to see the answers.

Story

Presentation

Poem

Photo

Movie

Web page

Song

Web browser

Music player

Video player

Picture editing program

Slideshow program

Writing program

Storing and naming

When we save our work on a computer, it is saved as a file. We need to give our file a name that we can remember so that we can find it when we want to open it again.

When naming a file on a computer that other people have access to, we should call it something we will remember, and that won't be confused with anyone else's. For example: DataDuck_DucklingStory.doc.

There are different places on our computer where we can save our work. The Desktop is what we see when we turn on our computer. We can save our work here, but if there are lots of files it gets messy – a bit like your bedroom if you don't put your toys away!

DATA DUCK
I like to include my name and information about what's inside my file.

There are other places that we can save our files. When we're at school, we might have a special folder with our name on it. We may also have special folders for saving certain types of stuff, like photos or music.

Remember, when saving files, think about what important information should be included so they can be found again.

The name game

Let's practise naming files. What would you call the following sorts of things? Where would be a good place to save them?

A story about your summer holidays.

A presentation about space.

A picture of a tree.

A web page about football.

Turn to page 76 to see the answers.

TOYS

BOOKS

Bits and bytes

The computer's brain (remember, it's called a 'processor'), will follow a program's instructions and work things out by turning little switches on and off.

The files and programs we store on computers are made up of 0s and 1s. The computer understands 0 and 1 because it knows 0 is off and 1 is on.

For example, if we were to tell a computer to write the letter A, the processor would store the letter as 01000001, because this is how the computer understands A.

Each 0 and 1 is called a 'bit'. Can you count how many bits there are in the letter A that the computer is storing?

A

01000001

DATA DUCK
When we store files, we need to think about the amount of space they take up in the computer's memory because we don't want to run out of room!

The smallest unit of memory is a bit. 8 bits make **1 byte**.

1,000 bytes make **1 kilobyte (KB),** which is enough storage for a page of writing.

Which is the biggest?

Can you sort the following file sizes in order from smallest to biggest?

- 20 kilobytes (20 KB)
- 2 gigabytes (2 GB)
- 10 bytes
- 10 megabytes (10 MB)
- 500 kilobytes (500 KB)

Turn to page 76 to see the answers.

1,000 kilobytes make **1 megabyte (MB),** which is enough storage for a photo.

1,000 megabytes make **1 gigabyte (GB),** which is enough storage for a TV show.

1,000 gigabytes make **1 terabyte (TB),** which can store up to 4 million photos!

USB 3.0

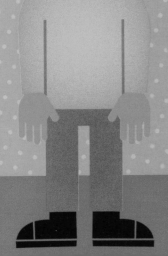

COMPUTER MEMORY

Searching and sorting

When we save a file, we store lots of information about that file at the same time. This means there is lots of information we can search for when we need to find the file again.

When we look for a book on a shelf, we look for the book title – but we might also look for the colour of the book or the picture on the front. It is the same when we look for computer files: there is lots of information we can use to help us search. This information is called 'metadata'.

Some of the information that will always be shown with the name of our file includes the date we made it, its size, where it is saved and its extension.

DATA DUCK

Remember, the 'extension' is the end part of a file name which shows the type of file that it is. We can sort and search by this information as well.

Sorting metadata

Can you work out the answers to the questions below using this file list?

What is the newest file?

What is the biggest file?

What is the smallest file?

Turn to page 76 to see the answers.

Name	Date modified	Size	Kind
AstronautStory.doc	Today 13:54	100 KB	Microsoft Word document
Penguins.jpg	11 August 16:19	3.3 MB	JPEG image
Timetable.xls	2 March 14:16	11 KB	Microsoft Excel workbook
Chapter2.pdf	7 November 11:08	230 KB	Adobe PDF document
My Stuff	Yesterday 09:37	- -	Folder
FlyingAKite.mov	6 February 17:49	47 MB	QT movie

Pixel perfect

Let's look at some of the ways a computer stores the pictures we view on it, and how programs read the information to show us pictures.

When we look at pictures on a computer screen, we are actually looking at millions of little dots called 'pixels'. These pixels can be turned on or off, and every single one can show us millions of colours.

Each one of these pixels has a specific location on the screen. For example, in this image, the pixel in the very top left of the grid might be called 0,0 whilst another one towards the middle of the screen might be called 6,8.

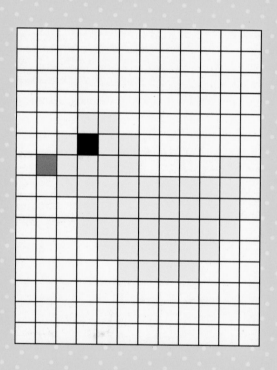

When we save a picture file, we save the colour and location for every pixel. When a picture program opens a photo file it reads the information stored there.

On and off

Imagine you have a computer screen that can only show black and white pictures. Its pixels can either be on (white) or off (black).

Data Duck has been a bit sneaky and turned on some pixels that he shouldn't have!

On a piece of paper, write down the number of each of the pixels you need to turn off to complete the smiley face.

Turn to page 76 to see the answers.

DATA DUCK
Remember, when we turn a pixel off, it goes black.

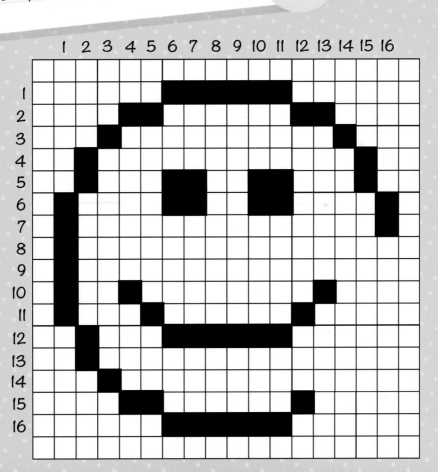

In the movies ...

Now that we understand how computers show us pictures, we can start to find out what we can do with pictures.

A video is a set of thousands of pictures that are shown very, very quickly one after the other.

When we look at a video, we are looking at 30 different pictures shown every single second. When we look at pictures that are shown very quickly one after the other, it looks like the images in the pictures are moving.

What is happening at 00:03:20?
What is happening at 00:03:40?

00:03:10

00:03:20

00:03:30

00:03:40

DATA DUCK
Don't forget that videos also have sound! When the computer plays a video, it knows exactly which sound should be played with each picture.

Make a flipbook

Let's have a look at how pictures can change using a flipbook.

Divide an A4 piece of paper into eight by folding it in half, then half again, and then in half again. Unfold it so it lies flat, then cut the paper along the fold lines so that you have eight pieces.

Draw a picture of a rocket on the first piece of paper. Then, draw the rocket again on the second piece of paper, slightly more to the right. Keep drawing a rocket on each piece of paper, moving it to the right each time.

Now, put all of the pieces together in order from first to last. Fix them together on the left edge and flip quickly through the pages. You've made your first flipbook!

Can you make another flipbook to create a story?

Sound it out

Now that we understand how pictures and videos are made, we can look at another type of content: sound!

Have you ever seen a funny picture that looks like this?

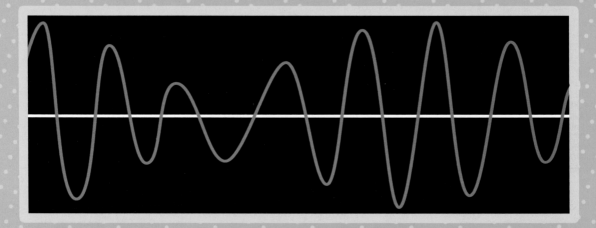

This is how a computer understands sound. The lines going up and down are called 'sound waves'. The waves that are taller will make a louder sound, while shorter waves will be quieter. Waves that are close together are high notes, while waves that are further apart are lower notes.

We can use the computer to change sounds too, such as noises we record with a microphone or songs that we save to our computer.

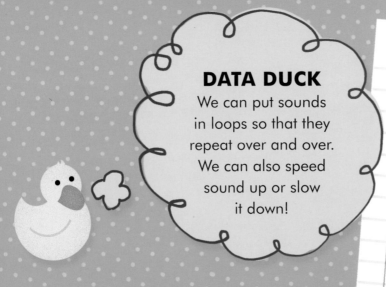

DATA DUCK

We can put sounds in loops so that they repeat over and over. We can also speed sound up or slow it down!

Decode the wave

Below is a sound picture showing different sorts of waves.

Which waves are the lowest notes? Which waves would make the loudest sound? Which waves would make the quietest sound?

Turn to page 76 to see the answers.

Go to **www.blueshiftcoding.com/ kidsgetcoding** to try out a sound editing exercise!

Staying safe online

I'm going to help you learn all about how to use the Internet safely when you travel through the digital world.

In order to be crafty coders in the future, we need to learn how to be Internet Superheroes who explore lots of incredible places online and keep our private information safe and away from strangers.

DATA DUCK

The Internet is a very big place. How do we find our way around?

DATA DUCK

Here are some key terms you will learn in this section. Try saying them out loud:

Internet

browser

URL

username

IP address

World Wide Web

cookies

search engine crawling

cyberbullying

What is the Internet?

The Internet is a gigantic network of computers that are all connected together. It lives on digital devices around the world.

These computers can be very big and powerful, or much smaller like a phone. Computers connected to the Internet use it to send little packages of information (called 'data') to one another. We can think of it like a very, very fast postal service!

DATA DUCK

We can view some of the information on the Internet as web pages. These web pages make up the World Wide Web.

Internet city

The way the Internet and World Wide Web work together is like a city. The roads are the Internet cables connecting everything together. The buildings are all the computers, big and small. The vehicles that travel on the roads, such as cars, are the information (web pages) moving around. Let's have a go at creating our own Internet city!

Instructions:
1. Draw a road network on some paper.
2. Add some buildings.
3. Draw a truck.
4. Draw a car.
5. Draw a motorcycle.
6. Draw a bicycle.

Use different colours to help you understand your Internet city: green for what represents Internet cables, red for what represents computers and blue for what represents web pages.

HELLO WORLD

Browsing the Web

To find what you are looking for on the World Wide Web, you need to use a special program on your computer or phone called a web browser.

Some popular web browsers are Chrome, Safari, Firefox, Internet Explorer and Opera. A browser can find and show content on the World Wide Web, including web pages, images and videos.

All the web pages on the Internet have a specific address, which is how we find them. This is known as a URL (or Uniform Resource Locator). The address for Google is www.google.com.

URLs get more complicated when we go beyond the home page of a website.

When we type each part of the URL into an address bar, we are helping to direct the browser to a specific web page.

https://www.hachettechildrens.co.uk/books/detail.page?isbn=9780750297028

The name of the way web pages are sent to your computer. The 's' at the end means it has been sent securely

World Wide Web

Company, school or organisation

Extension showing the home country or type of organisation

Section of the website the page is stored in

The specific web page – the '?' means it has come from a database

Build a URL

Imagine you are building a web page for yourself on the blueshift website. On a piece of paper, can you put the blocks below into the right order to make a correct URL?

Try typing this address into your browser. What do you find?

Turn to page 76 to see the answers.

#activity.html

www.

http://

kidsgetcoding/

blueshiftcoding.

internetsafety/

com/

DATA DUCK

We are 'online' when we are connected to the Internet. Our computer, phone or tablet needs some sort of connection to see pages through a web browser.

These are some of the pictures that your computer or phone might display if it is online.

((4G))

Search engines

Because there is so much 'stuff' on the Internet, we often need help finding things. A search engine helps us to find web pages that contain the information we need.

A search engine, like Google, uses a sort of robot called a 'crawler' to go through all the web pages on the Internet. The crawler looks at the content and keeps a record of all the words it finds.

These words are then sorted and organised into an 'index', which is like an enormous catalogue. When we search for something using the search engine, it will use the index to create a list of results for us.

DATA DUCK
There are over a TRILLION individual pages on the Web and that number is growing every day!

Higher or lower

A search engine uses certain steps to sort through information, just like a computer programmer uses an algorithm when they're writing code.

Let's imagine some of the steps a search engine might use to find information in an index. Ask someone to think of a number from one to eight. Follow the questions below to find their number in three guesses or less!

Can you see a pattern in the way the questions are asked?

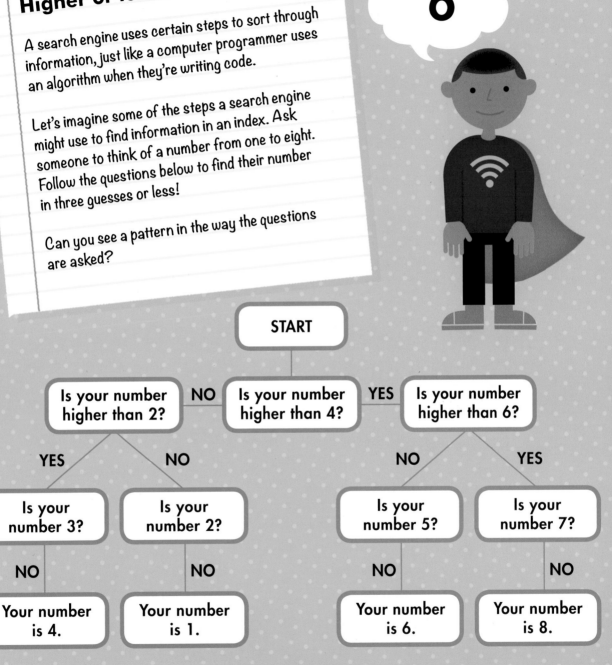

START

Is your number higher than 2? — **NO** — Is your number higher than 4? — **YES** — Is your number higher than 6?

YES / **NO**

Is your number 3?

Is your number 2?

NO — Your number is 4.

NO — Your number is 1.

NO / **YES**

Is your number 5?

Is your number 7?

NO — Your number is 6.

NO — Your number is 8.

Cookies!

Web pages use 'cookies' to keep track of us online. Every time we visit a web page, a cookie stores this information, and it begins to build up a picture of our online behaviour.

A cookie is a little piece of information that a website sends to our computers. It then sends back information to the website about us, such as what we click on and how much time is spent on the website.

Cookies can sometimes make it easier for us to use a website. For example, if we are shopping, cookies will help the website to provide information about things we might like to buy.

DATA DUCK

The first time we visit a website, a cookie is downloaded on to our computer browser that records how we used the site. The next time we visit that website, our browser checks to see if it has a cookie from that site already. If it does, the browser sends the cookie back to the website to help it remember us, and to be updated with new information.

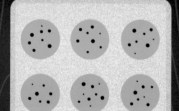

Cookie trail

It's important to remember that cookies keep track of what you do online.

Hansel is dropping bits of chocolate chip cookies at some sites. Gretel is dropping bits of peanut butter sandwich at other sites.

Which sites do they both like? Which sites does only Gretel visit?

Turn to page 76 to see the answers.

KidsReads

CBBC

Pottermore

NASA Kids' Club

Art Games

Club Penguin

Going places

We can use the Internet to visit lots of websites online. We can do our shopping, get directions to a museum or watch a football match.

The web pages we can look at online come from all around the world and are created by many different computer programmers. This means we have to stay safe online, just as we do in the 'real world'.

In the real world, we wouldn't go to places we are unsure about and we wouldn't give strangers our name and address.

It's important to always tell a grown up you trust if you see something online that you're unsure about. It is also a good idea to use your computer when a grown up is nearby, so that you can ask them questions easily about the things you do online.

All computers and other digital devices that are connected to the Internet have their own address called an IP (Internet Protocol) address. An IP address has four groups of numbers and looks something like this: 10.98.242.173.

What would you do ...

- if you saw something online that made you upset or uncomfortable?

- if you were online and a strange, flashing window popped up asking you to click on it?

- if you were on a web page and it asked you for your name?

- if someone said something mean about a picture you put online?

Turn to page 76 to see the answers.

DATA DUCK

IP addresses show people the country and city your device is in, and the way you are accessing the Internet. You can discover your IP address by typing 'IP address' into Google.

130.26.153.33

Keep it private

Sometimes we go to websites and we are asked to give information about ourselves.

Websites are usually built by people we don't know, and it's these people who are asking us questions. It's important not to reveal private information to strangers.

If you are ever unsure about which information you should give out online, just ask yourself if you would give it to a stranger in the real world.

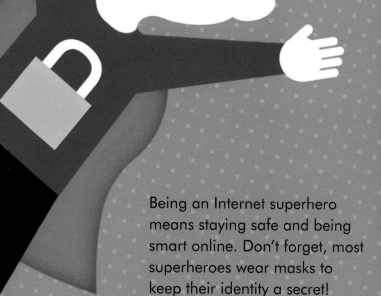

Being an Internet superhero means staying safe and being smart online. Don't forget, most superheroes wear masks to keep their identity a secret!

Be a real Internet superhero!

Below is a form from a shopping website online. To be an Internet Superhero you should only fill out the parts that keep your secret identity safe!

On a piece of paper, write down which pieces of information you think you should give.

Turn to page 76 to see the answers.

SHOP ONLINE   Toys   Games   Books   **My Basket**

Your name	
Your school's name	
Your pet's name	
Your parents' names	
Your birthday	
Your favourite colour	
Your parents' email address	
Your favourite sports team	
A picture of you	
Your parents' phone number	
Your address	

Our digital identity

Our digital identity is all the information about us that is on the Web. It is made up of everything that we put online.

Every time we post a photo or video, or write something, it makes up part of our digital identity. Once it is stored somewhere on the Internet, it may not ever be possible to delete it.

DATA DUCK

All the data we put online about ourselves is like a tattoo. It is a permanent collection of information about us, available online for others to find.

Lisa Smith 7th April

My mum baked me an amazing cake for my birthday today!

So far we've learnt about three ways information about us can get stored online:

- Cookies
- IP addresses
- Information you put into forms on web pages

What do you think the cookies, IP addresses and forms you have used say about you?

Even when we are careful not to put too much personal information on one website, if we post different things across lots of websites, someone can still gather that information together to find out who we are.

Putting clues together

Dotted around these two pages are things posted by somebody on different websites. Write a paragraph about what you have learnt about them from the information they have posted. Can you see how easy it is to form a picture of someone's life by what they leave online?

LisaMovieQueen:
Funny films are my favourite. This was SO good, and the main character looks just like me!

Amazing goal by Freddy Footwork

LisaMovieQueen:
What a great game! I'm so lucky that Birmingham United are my home team.

Super security!

The Internet wouldn't be any fun if we had to keep everything private. The best thing about the Internet is that it allows us to share information with our friends and see really exciting stuff.

When we post things like our work or pictures of ourselves on a website, we should ask ourselves some questions:

Who can see the website?

Kids and adults from my school only

I can post! (If in doubt, ask a grown up.)

Kids and adults from anywhere

Make sure you adjust the privacy settings on your page, so that only your friends can see it.

Many public websites have 'privacy settings' that allow us to say what's private and what's public.

We should always adjust the privacy settings on any new websites we join or apps we download.

Privacy settings

Who can see my stuff?

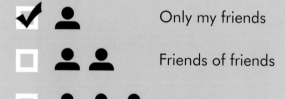

✔ 👤 Only my friends

☐ 👤👤 Friends of friends

☐ 👤👤👤 Everyone

Websites will often ask us if we have an account and to 'log in'. This means that we need a username and password to access the site's main information.

It is important that we make up usernames and passwords that we can remember. Don't use the same ones every time and never give away a superhero password. It's a secret!

DATA DUCK
Most of the time, anyone can see your username – so it's important to use one that does not give away your superhero identity!

My secret names and passwords

Can you think of some good usernames? Write down five on a piece of paper.

What secret passwords can you think of? Make sure they can't be guessed! Try to use letters and numbers in your password. Write down your top five!

For some help making secret passwords go to: **www.blueshiftcoding.com/kidsgetcoding** for our top secret password creator.

Sharing is caring

There are lots of websites that kids and adults use to share information with each other. These sorts of websites are called 'social media' websites.

A social media website is one where we have an account and we can share information about ourselves. Some of these websites are Facebook, Twitter and Instagram.

Most social media websites are only for people who are 13 and over. Many websites will ask us for our birthday before we sign up to them, to make sure that we do not see things that are not meant for kids.

DATA DUCK
We can connect with friends and strangers on social media websites. This means we should be very careful about who we make our 'friend' on a social media site and whether we know and can trust them. Sometimes baddies are hiding their real identity and aren't actually who they say they are!

Sometimes, people say mean things online. This is called 'cyberbullying'. When we see something online that worries us, we should always tell a grown up.

Internet superheroes know that they shouldn't say things to people online if they wouldn't say them in person.

Careful commenting

Data Duck posted a picture on his school website and lots of his classmates commented back. Here are some of the things that people wrote:

Term dates   **News**   **Picture Gallery**

 ProudGeek87   You have stinky feet!

 FootballFan4Eva   That's a really cool picture.

 BookLover12   I like how you drew the flower.

 TimeToShine   You are my best friend.

Draw a picture of how you think Data Duck would feel when he read these comments.

Words to remember

algorithm   a simple set of instructions that tells a computer what to do.

animate   to give the appearance that something on screen has come to life.

bit   the smallest unit of memory on a computer (it is equal to "0" or "1").

browser   the program we use to access the World Wide Web.

bug   a mistake in a computer program.

byte   8 bits.

code   the arrangement of instructions in a computer program.

condition   a factor that affects the instructions of a computer program.

cookies   packets of information that keep track of your online behaviour.

co-ordinates   a system of finding a position. Co-ordinates are made up of two numbers or letters: one representing the horizontal position, the other the vertical position.

cyberbullying   bullying that happens on the Internet.

debugging   to find and remove bugs or errors in a computer program.

extension   a part that is added to something.

file   the name given for something used to store information on a computer.

input   something that puts information into a computer, such as a mouse.

Internet   a giant network of computers that are all connected together.

IP address   four groups of numbers that make up an address that identifies a computer or digital device connected to the Internet.

kilobyte	1,000 bytes.
loop	a series of steps with the final step connected to the first step, so the steps are repeated.
megabyte	1,000 kilobytes.
memory	a means of storing information in a computer.
metadata	information about other information. For example, information about a file on a computer (such as date created and type of file).
output	something used to send information out of a computer, such as a printer.
pixel	a small dot used on a computer screen to display text or images. It can be turned on or off and given one of a number of millions of colours.
search engine	when robots called crawlers travel from web page to web page, keeping track of the information they find.
sequence	a particular order in which steps follow one another.
syntax	the structure of statements in a computer language.
URL	the address of a specific website.
username	the name you are known by on a website where you have an account.
variable	something that can be changed or adapted.

Activity answers

Page 7

There are 5 computers on this page: TV, phone, tablet, computer and stereo. Many TVs and stereos have little computer brains in them that allow them to find and play channels and programmes.

Page 13

For example: wake up; get dressed; eat breakfast; brush hair; brush teeth; put on shoes and jacket; pick up school bag.

Page 15

1. Heat oven to correct temperature.
2. Mix together the butter and sugar, then add in eggs and flour.
3. Grease baking tray.
4. Put spoonfuls of mixture onto tray, then bake for 10 minutes.
5. Turn off oven.
6. Eat and enjoy!

Page 17

Mechanic – Fixing Cars.
Cook – Tasty Dishes.
Builder – How to Build a House.
Doctor – Medical Dictionary.

Page 19

All the languages use the text Hello, World!
HTML uses brackets < > and forward slashes /.
Python uses brackets ().
Java uses a variety of brackets: [] {} ().
Scratch uses building blocks rather than symbols.

Page 21

Cold meat-free meal: cheese sandwich.
Cold meal with meat: ham and potato salad.

Page 23

1. Costume – Data Duck is wearing a hat.
2. Position – The mouse and Data Duck have switched places.
3. Rotation – The mouse is now facing the opposite direction.
4. Size – The mouse is now smaller.

Page 25

In the least number of moves:
Challenge 1: Move right 10 squares, move up 10 squares.
Challenge 2: Move up 2 squares, move right 7 squares, move right 2 squares, move right 1 square, move up 8 squares.
Challenge 3: Move right 9 squares, move up 2 squares, move left 2 squares, move left 2 squares, move up 8 squares, move right 5 squares.
Challenge 4: Move right 7 squares, move up 2 squares, move up 3 squares, move left 4 squares, move up 2 squares, move up 3 squares, move right 7 squares.

Page 27

The food is at $x=180$, $y=120$.
The bowl is at $x=0$, $y=-120$.
The dog is at $x=240$, $y=0$.

Page 28

You need the following steps:
Go to $x=120$, $y=-180$
Pick up basket
Go to $x=120$, $y=0$
Put apple in basket (this step will be needed three times)
Go to $x=-240$, $y=-60$
Go to $x=-180$, $y=120$

Page 31

Data Duck has drawn a square!

Page 33

'Put on pyjamas' has been used twice in the algorithm.

'Turn off light' is before 'Read story' in the algorithm.

Page 34

The Python program will draw a triangle.
The boat in the Scratch program will glide back and forth across the screen.

Page 35

The third instruction asks 'What's your age?' not 'What's your name?'

The fourth instruction says 'repeat 10 times' not 'forever'.

The fifth instruction says 'turn 51 degrees' not 'turn 15 degrees'.

The sixth instruction says 'move −10 steps', not 'move 10 steps'.

Page 39

Playing a game -- we are using the controller to move our players: INPUT

Writing a story: INPUT

Watching a movie: OUTPUT

Taking a photo: INPUT

Listening to music: OUTPUT

Printing a story: OUTPUT

Page 41

Story: writing program
Presentation: slideshow program

Poem: writing program
Photo: picture editing program
Movie: video player
Web page: web browser
Song: music player

Page 43

The name for each file should explain what it is. You should put it in a place that makes sense, either in a folder belonging to you, or in a folder for that type of file.

If you are sharing a folder with other people, you should include your name in the filename. For example, if Data Duck was sharing his folder with other ducks, he might write: DataDuckSummerStory. doc and save it in the 'Stories' folder on his school computer.

Your answers might be a bit different, but your filenames could have been:

SummerHoliday.doc, saved in Stories folder
Tree.jpeg, saved in Pictures folder
SpacePresentation.ppt, saved in Schoolwork folder
FootballWebPage.html, saved on the Desktop.

Page 45

10 bytes, 20 kilobytes, 500 kilobytes,10 megabytes, 2 gigabytes.

Page 47

Newest file: AstronautStory.doc
Biggest file: FlyingAKite.mov
Smallest file: Timetable.xls

Page 49

(13,15), (14,14), (15,13), (15,12), (16,11), (16,10), (16,9), (16,8).

Page 53

The C waves are the lowest notes.

The A waves would make the loudest sound.

The B waves would make the quietest sound.

Page 59

http://www.blueshiftcoding. com/kidsgetcoding/ internetsafety/#activity.html

Page 63

Both Hansel and Gretel visit NASA Kids' Club.

Only Gretel visits Pottermore and Club Penguin.

Page 65

1. If you see something online that makes you upset or unsure, you should talk to a grown up you trust.

2. If a strange flashing window appears on your screen, you should tell a grown up. Some content that is sent through the Internet is not appropriate for children and may contain nasty messages!

3. If in doubt, do not give your name to anyone online.

4. If someone says something mean about a picture you post online, you should tell a grown up. Cyberbullying is never okay.

Page 67

It's safe to give out your favourite colour or your sports team. It may be okay to give out your pet's name, as long as you don't give away any other information about where you live or parks you play in. You shouldn't give out anything else. Remember, the more pieces of information you give, the more strangers can form a picture of who you are.

Extension activities

Go to **blueshiftcoding.com/kidsgetcoding** for more fun activities and to practise:

- creating algorithms
- using variables
- using loops
- predicting what programs will do
- writing programs
- co-ordinates
- creating IF statements
- debugging
- creating and editing pictures, games, videos and sound files
- making pixel pictures
- creating flip books to tell a story

Index

Kids Get Coding: Algorithms and Bugs
first published in 2016 by Wayland
Kids Get Coding: Learning to Program
first published in 2016 by Wayland
Kids Get Coding: Our Digital World
first published in 2016 by Wayland
Kids Get Coding: Staying Safe Online
first published in 2016 by Wayland

This edition published in in 2016 by Wayland

Editors: Annabel Stones and Liza Miller
Illustration: Alex Westgate
Designer: Anthony Hannant (LittleRedAnt)

ISBN: 978 1 5263 0101 7
10 9 8 7 6 5 4 3 2 1

FSC
www.fsc.org

MIX
Paper from
responsible sources
FSC® C104740

Wayland
An imprint of
Hachette Children's Group
Part of Hodder & Stoughton
Carmelite House
50 Victoria Embankment
London EC4Y 0DZ

An Hachette UK Company
www.hachette.co.uk
www.hachettechildrens.co.uk

Printed in China

The website addresses (URLs) included in this book
were valid at the time of going to press.
However, it is possible that contents or addresses
may have changed since the publication of this
book. No responsibility for any such changes can
be accepted by either the author or the Publisher.